Sweet Pears and Sour Apples

Claudia Zeng

Presentation by *BookLeaf Publishing*

Web: www.bookleafpub.com

E-mail: info@bookleafpub.com

ISBN: 9789357691055

First edition 2022

DEDICATION

To my dearest family, beautiful friends and
those who happen to find and read my words...

love note to self

i'll open my heart to you
if you leave your daggers at the door
i'll warm your cold hands with a cup of tea
sit beside you for company
and in your own time
when you've drank every last drop
when your cup is empty
i'll refill it
i won't overpour

lost & found

from the edge of the world...
...i'll find you in every corner

bring my heart back down to earth

bring my heart back down to earth
please
it's been on the moon since the second your eyes
landed on mine
at 10:15pm on the 25th of july
gravity politely declined
it took my head but left my affections behind

my head is now back down on earth
but
my heart on the moon is insistently sending neon
signs
of love shining the brightest lights that occupy
the mind
blinding thoughts of reason over time
sensible judgement in a bind

bring my heart back down to earth
please
or my head would ask all of my sanity and sense
to resign
to surrender every logicality of mine
my heart on the moon should not be difficult to
find
for tonight, all stars are aligned

in the absence of me

in the absence of
me i'll look infinitely
to come and find you

forever

for the first time
we saw eachother we knew
this is forever

honeymoon eyes

the honeymoon phase
where soft eyes gaze longing
for the blushing face

a ghost love story

you want to hear me
express my love but you can
no longer see me

wallflower

i want to listen
but you won't talk

i want to talk
but you won't listen

now I listen
but i don't believe

i talk quietly
but i'm not shy

I'm not shy
I want to be unseen

the worst idea

you planted the worst idea in my head:

that we would be good together...

judge me for all that i am or not at all

judge me not by the colour of my hair
or the smoothness of my skin
by the sharpness of my eyes
or the shape of my chin
judge me not by the way i question
or the sound of my talk
by the bluntness of my answer
or the honesty of my thoughts
judge me not by the smoothness of my hair
or the colour of my skin
by the shape of my eyes
or the sharpness of my chin
judge me not by the sound of my question
or the way that i talk
by the honesty of my answer
or the bluntness of my thoughts

judge me for all that i am or not at all

acceptance

i survived your betrayal of my kindness
my willingness to accept all that is you
as long as you did with all that of me
but it is difficult to love when you are unsure
maybe the uncertainty should have been
recognised sooner as the answer
to my burning questions of why
you would or would not do
the things that you did or did not do
and i asked and asked and asked you
but the only answer you gave me was

silence

untitled love poem

whoever says ignorance is bliss really doesn't
know...
that it's better to have loved than not at all...

a world of fools

a world of fools
chasing after meaning of words
importance of nuances
a mindless flow in a stream of normality
a hopeless search for endless clarity
seeking the unreachable perfection beyond

thoughts on a train

in the eyes of a stranger
who am i?
a lonesome soul with a vacant gaze
not in sadness but
perhaps in a muddled haze
no.
in a light daze
watching raindrops throw themselves against the
train
magnetic attraction towards the pane
minute reflections of such vacant gaze
streaming downwards in hundred violently in
diagonal lanes
leaving nothing by the darkness and the grey
above where heavy clouds and sombreness lay

as i walked through the open door
and put my bags slowly on the floor
a warm voice from a room away
asks did you have a good day
a question from mother to daughter with no
delay
to which daughter to mother replies
unsure if it's the truth or a lie
good thank, everything is okay

message unsent

the beginning was so easy
you made me laugh and said that you liked me
caught me in a dream of a future you made see

i'm sorry i didn't know you were hurt before
you didn't tell me so how was i supposed to
know?
but why would you break me, like how she
broke you?
how could you even when you know the truth
that she loved you less than i do

i never asked if you'd like me to stay
'cause i didn't want to push you away
you would deny that you wanted me to
but i'm not the one and you always knew

i think we danced but i can't remember

at a wedding by the sea
on top of the cliff a guest quietly
approached and shouted in my ear
the music so loud i couldn't hear
i nodded politely though still unclear
and now the guest stood very near
... dance? i think i heard the word
as the guest flapped around like a bird
this confused bird i went and followed
i'll tell him i don't remember tomorrow

remind me when i want to
listen again

overthinking misfortunes from the past
how long does this misery last?
in the mind where painful memories manifest
struggling to decide what is best
for your present and your future
would you ever let another
in to feel your soul
your heart of gold?
it is difficult
but not impossible

sweet pears and sour apples

live your life tasting
the sweetest pears and the most
sourest apples